AWESOME SKATEBOARD

Tricks & Stunts

by Lori Polydoros

Reading Consultant:
Barbara J. Fox
Reading Specialist
North Carolina State University

Content Consultants:

Drew Mearns
Executive Director
Action Sports Alliance

Mimi Knoop
Co-Founder
Action Sports Alliance

CAPSTONE PRESS
a capstone imprint

Blazers is published by Capstone Press,
151 Good Counsel Drive, P.O. Box 669, Mankato, Minnesota 56002.
www.capstonepub.com

Books published by Capstone Press are manufactured with paper
containing at least 10 percent post-consumer waste.

Library of Congress Cataloging-in-Publication Data
Polydoros, Lori, 1968–
   Awesome skateboard tricks and stunts / by Lori Polydoros.
      p. cm.—(Blazers. Big air)
   Includes bibliographical references and index.
   Summary: "Describes extreme big-air stunts and tricks performed by professional
skateboarders"—Provided by publisher.
   ISBN 978-1-4296-5409-8 (library binding)
   1. Skateboarders. I. Title.
GV859.8.P65 2011
796.22—dc22   2010032196

Editorial Credits
Aaron Sautter, editor; Tracy Davies and Kyle Grenz, designers;
   Eric Manske, production specialist

Photo Credits
Alamy/Wig Worland, 16, 23
Corbis/NewSport/Ben Burgeson, 5
Getty Images Inc./Doug Pensinger, 27; Jeff Gross, 9; WireImage/Philip Schulte, 24
Newscom, cover, 13, 19; Icon SMI/Ric Tapia, 14, 20; Icon SMI/Tony Donaldson, 6, 11, 29

Artistic Effects
iStockphoto/Guillermo Perales, peter zelei, 4x6

The publisher does not endorse products whose logos may appear
in images in this book.

Printed in the United States of America in Stevens Point, Wisconsin.

092010   005934WZS11

TABLE OF CONTENTS

Spinning, Grinding, and Flying High!

Professional skateboarders love doing **ollies** and stunts. They love catching big air too. The best riders do difficult moves while soaring high in the air.

FACT:
Alan "Ollie" Felfand created the Ollie on a ramp in the late 1970s. Rodney Mullen was the first to pop an Ollie on flat ground.

ollie—a skateboarding move in which the board is popped into the air by the rider's feet

Frontside Grind

In a Frontside Grind, the rider flies up the **half-pipe** facing frontside. At the top, he grinds the back truck on the ramp's lip. Scrape! Then he turns and drops back down into the ramp.

half-pipe—a U-shaped ramp with high walls

MUTE AIR

The **Mute** Air is a fun and stylish trick. The rider flies off the ramp frontside. While in the air, she grabs the board mute. She also stretches out her arm for extra style points.

FACT:
Doing a trick while facing the wall is called frontside. Backside means your back faces the wall.

mute—when a rider grabs the toeside of the board with the front hand

Fast Plant

A skater speeds up the half-pipe ramp frontside. At the last second, he grabs the board's nose. He takes his back foot off the board and lands on the ramp's lip. Then he jumps into the ramp again to finish off a great Fast Plant.

CROOKED GRIND

Crooked Grinds take perfect balance. The skater first hops up to a rail. He balances on the board's nose as he grinds the front truck. He angles the board's tail up and away from the rail.

FACT:
Grinding both sets of trucks is called a 50-50.

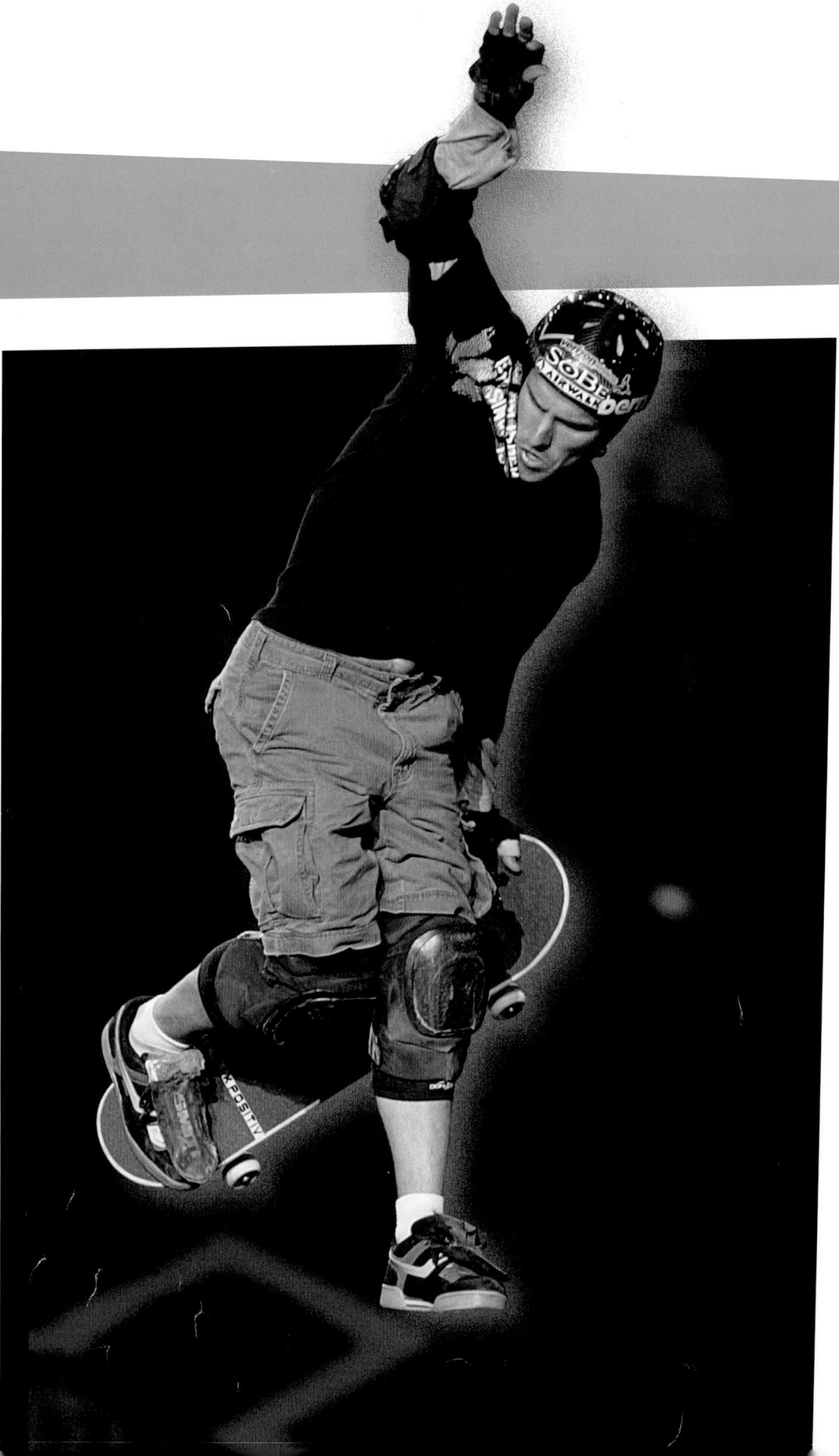
SoBe
AIR WALK

JUDO AIR

A Judo Air looks like a karate kick in midair! The skater flies off the ramp and grabs the board's nose. Then he pulls the board backward while kicking out his front foot.

FACT:
In an Anti-Judo Air, the rider kicks his leg out twice. He kicks once in front of the board and once behind before landing.

FACT:
Tony Hawk is the "King of Skateboarding."
He's won several X Games gold medals. He
has also created about 80 new tricks.

HEELFLIP VARIAL LIEN AIR

The skater flies into the air and **heelflips** the board. The board flips once and spins in a half-circle. The skater grabs the board between his legs and lands back on the ramp. He's just hit a perfect Heelflip **Varial** Lien Air!

heelflip—a move in which the rider flips the board over with his or her heel

varial—when a rider's body or the board turns 180 degrees while in the air

360 OLLIE MELON 540

Rob Lorifice first flies off the mega ramp. He does a full spin with no grabs to stick a 360 Ollie. Then he soars off a huge vertical half-pipe for a **melon** grab 540. He's like an acrobat tumbling in the air at amazing heights!

melon—when a rider grabs the heel side of the board with his or her front hand

FACT:
At the 2009 X Games, Rob Lorifice nailed a 360 Ollie Melon 540 to win a bronze medal.

Backside Fingerflip Air

Bob Burnquist is going for a Backside Fingerflip Air. He grabs the board's nose and kicks out his legs. He flips the board with his hand. Finally, he plants his feet back on the board to stick the landing!

FRONTSIDE FLIP

The rider races toward some stairs and pops into the air. He flicks the board with his front toe. It flips wildly under his feet as he spins in a half-circle. Finally, he connects with the board to land an incredible Frontside Flip.

Kickflip INDY

The best skaters make the Kickflip **Indy** look easy. While in the air, a skater flips the board with his foot. After it flips once, the skater grabs the board with his back hand. Then he pulls it back to his feet for the landing.

indy—when a rider grabs the toeside of the board with his or her back hand

540 MCTWIST

The 540 McTwist is a real crowd pleaser. The rider launches into the air backside. He grabs the board indy and does a full flip. At the same time, he spins in a half-circle. Then he lands smoothly back on the ramp.

FACT:
Mike McGill pulled off the first McTwist trick on a half-pipe in Sweden in 1984.

900

In the 1999 X Games, Tony Hawk tried for a 900. No one had ever landed the stunt. Hawk could spin two and a half times. But he couldn't stick the landing. On his eleventh try, he finally nailed it. The 900 helped him win the Best Trick event!

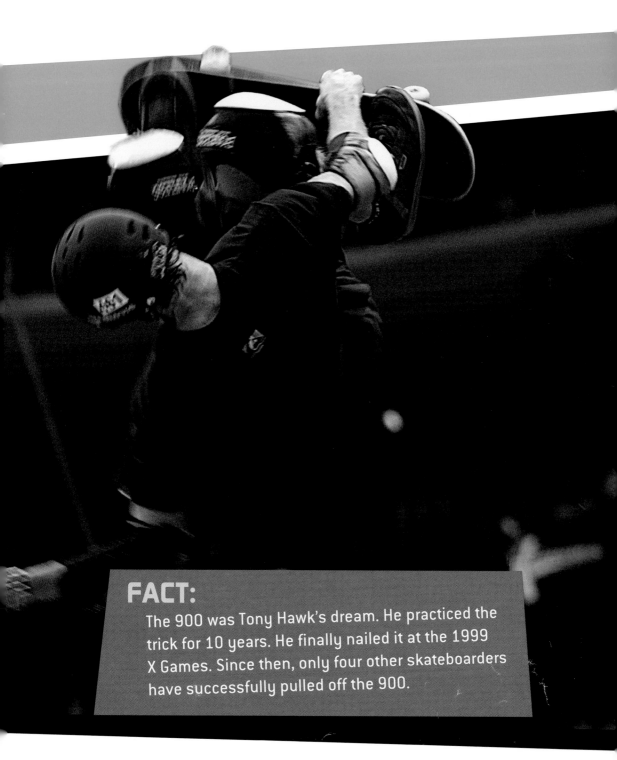

FACT:
The 900 was Tony Hawk's dream. He practiced the trick for 10 years. He finally nailed it at the 1999 X Games. Since then, only four other skateboarders have successfully pulled off the 900.

GLOSSARY

grind (GRINDE)—a skateboarding move in which one or both trucks slide across the surface of an object

half-pipe (HAF-pipe)—a U-shaped ramp with high walls

heelflip (HEEL-flip)—a skateboarding move in which the rider flips the board over with his or her heel

indy (IN-dee)—a grab in which the rider places his or her back hand on the toeside of the board

melon (MEL-uhn)—a grab in which the rider places his or her leading hand on the heel side of the board

mute (MYOOT)—a grab in which a rider places his or her leading hand on the toeside of the board

ollie (OL-ee)—a move where the rider pops the skateboard into the air with his or her feet

truck (TRUHK)—a metal axle that attaches the wheels to the skateboard

varial (VAYR-ee-uhl)—a move that involves either the rider's body or the board turning 180 degrees while in the air

READ MORE

Hocking, Justin. *Skateboarding Tricks and Techniques.* Power Skateboarding. New York: PowerKids Press, 2006.

Mattern, Joanne. *Skateboarding.* Action Sports. Vero Beach, Fla.: Rourke Publishing, 2009.

Miller, Connie Colwell. *Skateboarding Big Air.* X Games. Mankato, Minn.: Capstone Press, 2008.

INTERNET SITES

FactHound offers a safe, fun way to find Internet sites related to this book. All of the sites on FactHound have been researched by our staff.

Here's all you do:

Visit *www.facthound.com*

Type in this code: 9781429654098

Super-cool stuff! Check out projects, games and lots more at **www.capstonekids.com**

INDEX